ODYSSA RIVERA ABILLE

Like A New Sun Rising

A Collection of Poems on Love

First edition

Illustration by Ifrah Fatima
Editing by Sophia Elaine Hanson
Editing by Clara Abigail
Cover art by rainygraphic

This book was professionally typeset on Reedsy.
Find out more at reedsy.com

For Ben and Digna

For whole centuries of folly, noise and
sin!
Shut them in,
With their triumphs and their glories
and the rest!
Love is best.

Robert Browning

Contents

II   Volume Two

Acknowledgement

To Ben and Digna, for their unconditional love and support throughout the years. This book is for you. To Deo, Jaja, Dennis, and Dinah, thank you for being there. Sophia Hanson and Clara Abigail, thank you for hearing my voice and sharing your expertise. R.W. Harrison, I take all of your advice to heart. Andrew, I'm grateful for your encouragement from day one. Last, to the youngest, smallest members of our family, Peanut and Jackie, you fill our house with joy.

Prologue

Imagine going on a first date.

You see your date's face for the first time. You pull him to you for a quick hug or kiss, depending on what's acceptable. Throwing a big smile, you say, "It's nice to finally meet you."

You walk over to your seats, talk endlessly about jobs, hobbies, and the news. You size him up and wonder if you should go for another round of beer (or wine?) or pretend your mom needs you at home in the next ten minutes.

This book is our first meeting. I don't care about which gender pronouns you use, but let's pretend we're meeting for the first time. Now, this can turn out horribly. However, we can make this memorable through radical honesty. There's no way this relationship can work without it.

Author and neuroscientist Sam Harris shared a powerful message in his long-form essay book *Lying*. He said, "Honesty is a gift we can give to others. It is also a source of power and an engine of simplicity. Knowing that we will attempt to tell the truth, whatever the circumstances, leaves us with little to prepare for. We can simply be ourselves."

You and I – we cared too much, loved to the extreme, suffered in silence, stood at crossroads with no signposts. We stumbled our way to the paved road, wishing for an uneventful journey.

I saved and published these poems hoping to find one or a few hundred readers who, once, have felt and done the same or treaded the opposite path. Nothing could be more rewarding than finding a connection through one's work.

The heroine's story is the same each time: she suffers, fights her way into battle, survives more hardships, kills villains, and wins in the end. Each of us has our own heroic narrative, and even though the storyline is the same, the angle makes each extraordinary.

I wrote this book from the perspective of a woman in her twenties who found her way through work and business, sobbed in bed because she failed at both. Her preferred cafe was nearby, so she made a regular appointment to write poems because it was a better escape than drinking, partying, and crying.

At least she created something. She got by. That season ended. The hero story was complete. The verses were out of sight for the next seven years.

Writer Elizabeth Gilbert said, "The universe buries strange jewels deep within us all, and then stands back to see if we can find them."

There's a lot of searching and unpacking to do. Now my hidden treasures are out. If you're holding this book, you're here to slow down, sit, and remember with me. I'm delighted!

Make these words your own. Nibble on each story, if you may. Share it, give it away, pass it around. Let this book give you access to a range of emotions that only you feel and understand.

May this book dig deep into the past you buried alive, those you secretly long for and ponder in the late evenings.

May this book be your companion to a love that's enchanting, mysterious, and ever-changing. May this remind you of a love that once was, what it could have been, and how it turned out to be.

I

Volume One

Introduction

It was the relationship of my, and most girls', dreams. My family loved him — he was respectful (of utmost importance to Filipino parents), decent, came from a wonderful family, studied and worked hard, and had plans for our future. He was everything my parents and I hoped for.

It was a solid relationship until it stopped being one. He pursued further studies while working and at the same time, I left my job to start a business. Living in separate cities became a barrier for us. Aside from the Manila traffic, we just didn't have the energy to meet regularly, let alone go on dates and trips. Or we lacked reasons to do so.

The feelings gradually faded, and we grew apart. I wanted to explore things beyond my usual reach — business, travel, fitness. I had so much more to do, prove, and achieve. On top of preparing for our marriage, he was aiming for stability in his job by obtaining a higher degree.

The end of that relationship plunged me into unexplainable sadness for a long time. I went through what tree experts call a transplant shock. This happens to trees when they get uprooted from the ground. Trees get uprooted because of natural disasters, construction damage, and disease.

No matter how robust the roots, trunk, and branches are,

not all of them survive. Depending on the length of time the roots are exposed to air, the size of the tree, and the treatment they receive when transferred, they could die. Large trees with extensive roots are tougher to transplant than younger, smaller ones.

The first month without him was exceptionally painful. It felt as if I lost a limb. It disrupted my life in ways I couldn't count. After all, he was present in every aspect of my life — family, friends, church, work. We grew together, planned a life together. There was no life without him, and he was no longer there. I was a young tree who had been uprooted. To survive, I needed loads of nourishment — water, sunlight, healthy soil. I needed to grow new, healthy roots once more. Experts say transplanted trees thrive when roots are moist and given enough time to grow. The lesson? Learn to wait for healing and expansion.

This first set of poems talks about disillusionment, saying goodbye, moving from one home to the next, refusing change, and asking questions like, "What's out there for me?" When life turns upside down, remember: wounds heal, storms pass. Everything is temporary.

To Your Next Love

May she look at you in the morning
and watch you peacefully sleep.
Allow no fear, pain, nor sorrow
to catch you, terrify, or keep.

May she observe your chest so quietly
as it goes up, down with each breath.
Praise the One for the new dawn
and know His love knows no depths.

May she, too, look into your eyes
as you blink your first for the day.
May she love you like it's the end
and hold you like dying prey.

May she roll back into your arms
and make herself warm and at home.
Let you wrap her like a blanket
tangled in your limbs to own.

May she remain secretly wanting
no matter how hard it may seem.

Shield your beauty in a frame,
treat you like her king.

Goodbye

Uncovered a glorious mystery,
one that few have seen.
Trampled upon a new star,
a sun that's been in hiding.

Faith in love is renewed.
My eyes were blinded by the light.
The Scriptures tell a story
of a man, getting back his sight.

Indeed, the day has come
when planets must rearrange.
My world is about to shift.
The sun's coming out of the rain.

I must leave behind a story,
one that gave birth to a new past.
I look away and return to my space;
nothing on this earth lasts.

As I let the light fade slowly,
the twinkling gets darker in time.

My thoughts travel the globe,
wandering alone at night.

Descending from the moon, I go,
to surrender a discovery made.
Midst the smiles of men,
a tear would fall from pain.

Sunset

Leaping to a steady rock,
I put my trust in you.
Keeping my eyes forward,
my search has found its truth.

Anguish and comedy we make,
sentiments stirred with words.
A beautiful exchange
between strings and chords.

My instinct tells me
this won't last for long.
My mind's made calculations
of the lines from our song.

Between hello and goodbye,
there can be found a love.
That's what you and I have built.
It goes beyond and above.

Whenever questions linger,
I turn to your embrace.

Here is where I unearth
your captivating, glorious space.

Bracing myself in the dark,
learning to keep a straight face.
Quietly, we will end
and fall out from grace.

Saying "until we meet again,"
walking away with a smile.
The sun is now setting.
It was perfect for a while.

Drive

Looking to the front and back
while driving down a narrow road.
The blackness still surrounds me
like a sack of heavy stones.

The pretty smile is gone
and out comes the great sorrow.
The game is over now.
I have become my own foe.

This day marks the sad end
of a long-running show.
The beginning of a story
no one really knows.

This lead star who once soared high
is now stooping down below.
I've proven nothing for myself—
it's time for me to go.

Don't

Please don't come too close.
This heart does not know
how to remain mellow yet firm.
This heart might lose control.

Please don't tell me truths
that could turn into lies.
Your mind changes abruptly.
Tears fall fast from my eyes.

Please don't stare at me
for my hands and knees might shake.
Your stare has that impact,
the walls inside could break.

Please don't walk toward me
and suddenly fake a fall.
My strength cannot carry you
even if I give my all.

Please let me be alone
to live my life as I can.

Go be who you should be
without being called 'my man'.

Please don't say goodbye
when you decide to leave.
There is no looking back
when there's nothing to retrieve.

We Both Knew

So many what-ifs, my life has about the future, present, and past. Countless questions, I still ask "What is?" and "What was?"

I knew it was love. I knew it was true. But how come it never pushed through? The two of us were sure. We very well knew. We made ourselves shine on a night so blue.

Wasted Time

More wasted time, more wasted space,
scenes in my mind I can't erase.
Between tissue and skin are hate and hate,
questions without answers about my fate.

To places, I wander, look, and see
the mountains, the skies, my lover's plea.
His magic and wonders don't amuse me.
"Stop, my heart, and think of what could be."

Fingers are clasped tightly together.
The clouds above now go under.
White flags appear, a cue of surrender;
depression spreading like wild fire.

Confusion

A hundred questions linger in my mind.
What is it I'm trying to find?
Am I striving for what society decides?
Am I still looking for my heart's desire?

Every minute, a puzzle is formed.
My life unfolds, a new yesterday is born.
The present is shaken, many lives are torn.
We stumble, we stand, we arrive, we mourn.

War

Standing alone to make things right,
my desire is to hold a fight

for all the things I love so dear.
This new war must determine the steer.

The battlefield is full, soldiers are ready.
My shield is blessed, my heart is heavy.

Pacing the arena, I hit with all my might.
Blood spills on the ground with each blow and strike.

Until today, the fight has not ended.
I look to the day when the wounds are mended.

No triumph in this world can alter what I feel.
Winning alone has no power to heal.

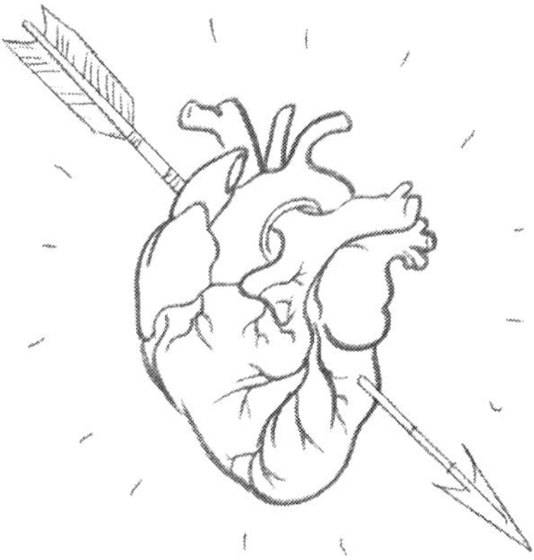

Regrets

My heart is scarred by my own words.
My hands are emptied by your loss.
My eyes are searching for the one
that gives an effect to a cause.

Teardrops resemble Niagara,
unstoppable, rapidly falling down.
Lips twist in a downward direction
careful not to make a sound.

In the still of the night
as this side of the world sleeps,
my thoughts travel to where you are,
wishing it was me you chose to keep.

Stupidity ruled my senses.
My tongue is the sharpest sword.
Hatred comes out of me like fire
from a place where no one is lord.

Regrets fill my heart and head.
Dead air is on the record.

Silence is as loud as a bomb
that was sent without a word.

Back To The Start

A sense of steadiness
washes over me
like the sun
blessing a praying tree.

The entire universe
seems to agree with me.
She nods with my desire,
to set this prisoner free.

About ten people
in the same place as I,
looking at two directions,
to live or to die.

Getting lost in this
thing called life
as if I'm standing
alone in the night.

Like a once clear rainbow,
fading away from afar,

little by little,
life again becomes art.

Though I see your image,
we are apart.
I turn my body away
to go back to the start.

My Heart

My heart is bursting for a love
who is many miles away.
There is a fire inside of me
and it burns a blue flame.

My heart is beating for a love
that can never be mine.
I only have the photographs
your pretty face left behind.

My heart is yearning for a love
that is wanted by many.
From left to right, here they come.
Bodies and words run aplenty.

My heart is aching for a love
that will remain a dream.
He will never mean what he says.
He will never say what he means.

My heart will continue to love
for my heart knows what is true:

There's no one else in the world
who can love you as I do.

Fade

Black turns to grey.
Strong wind becomes air.
Winter arrives again.
Somewhere gets nowhere.

Stories end, songs conclude.
Books are kept away.
Love runs out fast or slow,
melts like a heated clay.

The sun rises and sets again.
Children grow up and leave.
Dreams rise, then are forgotten—
some things you can't conceive.

Days turn into months.
Months turn into years.
But fading won't make me run
and turn my faith to fear.

Mirrors

Facing myself in the mirror,
my halo I no longer see.
Looking at my own reflection
wondering how the conclusion can be.

Tears begin to gather,
I try to stop their fall.
Remembering the old times
when you were still my all.

Lost time won't come back.
The clock's hands won't move.
Mem'ries can be replayed
but have nothing left to prove.

Thinking about my past,
I stare blankly at my face.
The lines have gone deeper.
Lines time cannot erase.

II

Volume Two

Introduction

A few years after the relationship ended, I did more. I learned new skills, got promoted at work, went back to dating. Then I started traveling by myself.

Using part of my savings, I bought plane tickets at discounted prices, couch-surfed, stayed in cheap hostels, ate street food, and split expenses with fellow travelers. I didn't care about scrimping — as long as I was out there, I was fine.

Instead of shopping for new clothes and shoes, I invested in a sturdy travel backpack, hiking shoes, sports gear, and items that would help me travel lighter and better.

It wasn't only the experiences I was after. Each trip came with a simple, practical lesson.

In Malaysia, a painfully shy Muslim woman rescued me from a van driver trying to rip me off. I learned a smile can go a long way.

In a canyoneering trip in the Philippines, the first jump off a cliff about six feet got my legs trembling like never before. I learned that indoor and outdoor climbing cannot take away one's fear of heights. You just have to jump.

In the Maldives, I met a Bangladeshi who went out of his way to prepare a birthday party for my partner. They only met once. I learned strangers can take you by surprise.

I fell deeply in love. There was nothing more I wanted but to feed myself with new travel experiences. I was hungry.

It was a time of adventure, courage, and restoration. The young tree that was uprooted years ago was growing. I was receiving the nourishment I'd always needed while on the road.

The years passed, and the passion for travel has waned. Now that I'm older, I travel for different reasons. It's no longer for adventure, but solitude. No longer for the adrenaline high, but the tranquility.

I am no longer soul-searching. I found stability and security in myself through the people I met and the places I visited.

Travel became the road to finding myself.

The next set of poems has a similar intensity. It's consuming, lustful, driven by impulse. Then it slows down like a Sunday drive through the countryside. It talks about a fierce love that, over time, changes into tenderness and warmth.

Worship

The rays of the sun
I can see through your eyes.
A picture of perfection.
I am mesmerized.

I hear the heavens sing
when you open your mouth;
like a choir of angels
ascended from the south.

The bridge of your nose
has nothing to compare.
Your scent is fragrant.
Let me catch some air.

I am held tight.
I am covered by a wall.
Your shoulders go on forever.
Your fortress cannot fall.

A chest as strong as a shield
protects my weakened state.

This army of one
can halt a losing fate.

Entwined between legs of steel,
I don't feel any pang at all.
One will choose to be here
to be present when you call.

Waking Up

This frail body
as fragile as mine
cannot hide away
its look of surprise.

The strength your arms
give away each time,
my heart can't manage
to escape and deny.

A year has passed,
the feelings are alive.
A wave still crashes
each time you walk by.

Even if I've known,
heard about your lies,
it sees only your eyes
that bid many a goodbye.

Fragrance is coming
from your faint sigh.

I waited so long
all my life

to hear you breathe
quietly at dawn
and hold your hand tight.
Victory is won.

Like A Child

I love for a reason that reason does not know. I love with no doubts, the dangers I forgo.

I love the joy of being complete and whole. I love with an endless passion that burns through one's soul.

I love through the rain when uncertainty shows. I love with gladness through all of life's blows.

I love like a child with an innocence unknown. I love to find a place I can call my own.

Up Close

For the first time I see you up close.
I can't peel my eyes off your face's glow.
I sense your wanting, from your moves, I know.
Give me a minute before I let go.

We say our first hello and I give you a kiss
for a brief connection as beautiful as this.
It carried me to a world of bliss.
A word to myself: *This I can't miss.*

Slowly, as the night unfolds, we move as one.
We sway back and forth like hell is done.
You go deep inside, and my doubts are gone.
The war is over; you have won.

I cry from agony, I cry from hunger
for more of your touch, I surrender.
Surely, the gods have made another wonder.
Right beside me, I found the answer.

I close my eyes to feel your hands
all over my body. Your touch is like sand,

smooth and lovely. Now, I understand
love is beyond owning a piece of land.

Sleep abounds our bed of crumpled sheets.
This moment - too vulnerable and sweet.
Serenity surrounds our dreams.
The end is far, that's how it seems.

Surrender

The valleys and rivers
of your body, I traverse.
Your touch has removed
the enduring curse.

I let my mouth
find its way to yours.
Without stopping,
it leads me to your door.

Explosions occur
one after the other.
It freezes like hard ice.
It's as hot as a raging fire.

We sway like branches,
move back and forth together.
The night is just starting;
I promise to surrender.

Dream

Haunted by the past,
I sleep alone at night.
Scenes play over in my head
as if I pressed rewind.

Emotions are stirred,
feelings remembered.
Thoughts invade my thoughts,
my sobs are spilling over.

Then I see an image
from up close. I see your face.
Like a new sun rising,
your lips are saying grace.

I take the comfort that I can,
as surreal as this might seem.
I need more hours in bed
not to wake up from this dream.

October

I will always look back
to that night in October.
A new life took over.
How greatly, I can't measure.

We get out of the car
to walk to the shore.
It is a wonderful night
to see what we are for.

The darkness is overwhelming.
The wind is blowing gently.
The sea is whispering its song.
There's no space for worry.

I start to rub your back
to extend to you my warmth.
It's still so hard to believe
that I have won your heart.

Here I am, looking at you
looking at me.

A love that stands this strong
is a love that stands so free.

The two of us make love.
There's a moment of bliss
when your round eyes closed
on a night like this.

Picture

I paint a picture of you
but the colors lack variety.
My eyes stare earnest
at this canvas so empty.

Your anger, your wonder,
your power and complexity.
It's hard to define you
without intensity.

Like a lamppost on the street
that lights up my face,
your presence is fuel
to these burning flames.

Your truths come with lies
but it's your word I believe.
Our hands fit perfectly
Like threads women weave.

To fill this empty space
is a mission I must achieve.

No rewards, no applause;
there is nothing I expect to receive.

Only through a painting
can I describe you away.
To freeze you in the moment,
seized to forever stay.

Us

People make history together.
You and I have made our own.
The world is our combat zone.
Beside each other is our home.

Countless battles we have fought,
against the odds and each other.
Each strike has left a mark.
Each shot has made us stronger.

Future

The roads will be bumpy,
the thunder will bring rain.
I will never be perfect.
I learned this the hard way.

Celestial bodies may not shine,
they may forget to appear.
The constellations may be covered,
but there's no reason to fear.

The darkness may loom
but only for a time.
The love you gave
I can only call mine.

You

Within the few years
I have spent alive,
never have I seen
a man who's willing to try.

How is it possible
to love a girl like me
when I know that it's as hard
as walking sea to sea?

The heavens are clear,
the clouds in full play.
Past the darkness,
closer to the day.

You shield me from a world
of uncertainty and grief.
You gave me a promise
To never, ever leave.

What Love Means

Love is not just a word.
It's something you do.
Love is never an excuse
or an empty "I love you."

Love is a quiet wave.
It's not something you scream.
Love paves a way
for two to make a team.

Love is an act,
not a question of who's who.
Love taunts facts,
shifting fake to truth.

Love is a whisper
to a voiceless, waiting crowd.
Love could be muted,
unmoving, still, but loud.

Love is the motion
that makes dominos fall.

Love is a mission
to hear a loved one's call.

Love pulls like gravity
when you're soaring high.
Love flies away
like an eagle taking flight.

Love gives without doubts,
shares without hesitation.
Love is unconditional
and lives with no expectations.

Love dances in the rain
and wipes the glass clear.
Love does not know time—
no second, hour, or year.

Promise

A legion of love stories
I have heard before.
Made up or true to life,
gossip, real or rumor.

These questions I have heard.
Now I ask you and I,
"Why do we cry? Why do we laugh?
How can we love then lie?"

Can one truly forgive
and forget the past?
When do you know
if a love is bound to last?

I am no genius.
I stare at the blank walls.
But I know when, how to ask
and to the angels I call.

We do not have to know
everything to be complete.

Being alive is enough
to get us back on our feet.

Let me say this to you,
my love for many years.
Ink will fade someday
but, forever, I will be here.

Painter

If only my hands can paint
abstract without definition.
My eyes can look at you all day,
to comprehend is a mission.

The colors of the palette
must be expressed on this wall
to paint what my eyes see.
This space is too small.

Sitting on a sturdy chair,
the strokes go left and right.
Hours and days I spend
to arrive at your wondrous sight.

Hanging for all to see,
trapping the hearts of many.
Smiling quietly to myself—
you and I just turned to *we*.

Let Me Be

Let me be the one
to hold you, dear.
When the night is cold,
I will keep you here.

Let me be the one
to touch your hand.
When chaos surrounds you,
I will understand.

Let me be the one
to catch your fall.
When you can't anymore,
I will stand tall.

Let me be the one
to look you in the eye
when we face each other,
and all we do is cry.

Let me be the one

to make the change.
When the world disappoints,
let me rearrange.

Let me be the one
to chase those troubles away.
When sadness abounds,
deliverance will come your way.

Perfect

This love cannot compete with any gift I have received.
No flashy lights, flaws, nor doubts can change what I believe.

Fantasy can't catch up with this reality we made.
Hand in hand, we stand together, brave to face a brand-new day.

About the Author

Odyssa Rivera Abille is the author of the newest poetry book, Like A New Sun Rising: A Collection of Poems on Love. She completed her Bachelor of Arts in Behavioral Science from the University of Santo Tomas in Manila, Philippines. Her work is featured in The Good Men Project, Girl Tell Me, and DoYou Yoga. She practices yoga, enjoys traveling, gets lost in books and Korean drama.

You can connect with me on:
- https://odyssawrites.com
- http://odyssa.medium.com
- http://instagram.com/odyssaa

Made in the USA
Middletown, DE
25 November 2021

53410990R00042